Bird Watchin
A Track And ı
For Birdwatchers

Dubreck World Publishing

Copyright

DUBRECK WORLD PUBLISHING

Dedicated to all
awesome birdwatchers,
young and old!

If found, please return to:

................MAX................................

Bird Log Summary

Date	Bird Seen
10.11.24	sky - lark

Date	Bird Seen

Date	Bird Seen
10.11.24	black bird

Date: 10th november Time: ✓ 3:08
Location: codden hill
Bird Species:
black-bird

Description:
A small black bird
with a orange beak.

Behaviour:
it was just flying
Through the sky it
goes very fast.

Sketch / Photo

Weather: cloudy

Habitat: fArmland

Notes: Nothing.

Date: 10th November Time: 3:20
Location: CoADen hill
Bird Species: 5ky - Lark

Description: Small bird flying high, tweeting.

Behaviour: flying around alot. and tweeting.

Weather: sunny with some clouds
Habitat: fArmlAnd

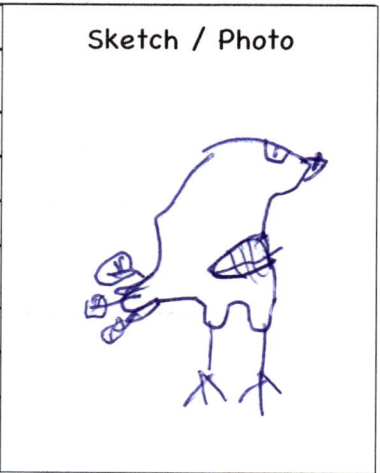

Notes: Nothing.

Sketch / Photo

8

Date: 10th November Time: 3:23
Location: codden hill
Bird Species: rook

Description: They were flying in a flock.

Behaviour: flying in groves.

Weather: sunny

Habitat: fArm land

Notes: Nothing

Sketch / Photo

Date:_____Time:_____

Location:_____

Bird Species:

_____

Description:

_____

_____

_____

_____

Behaviour:

_____

_____

_____

	Sketch / Photo
Weather:_____	
Habitat:_____	
Notes:_____	
_____	
_____	
_____	

Date:_____Time:_____

Location:_____

Bird Species:

_____

Description:

_____

_____

_____

_____

Behaviour:

_____

_____

_____

Weather:_____

Habitat:_____

Notes:_____

_____

_____

_____

Sketch / Photo

Date:_____Time:_____

Location:_____

Bird Species:

_____

Description:

_____
_____
_____
_____

Behaviour:

_____
_____

_____

	Sketch / Photo
Weather:_____	
Habitat:_____	
Notes:_____	

Date:_____Time:_____

Location:_____

Bird Species:

_____

Description:

_____

_____

_____

_____

Behaviour:

_____

_____

_____

_____

| Sketch / Photo |

Weather:_____

Habitat:_____

Notes:_____

_____

_____

_____

Date:_____Time:_____

Location:_____

Bird Species:

_____

Description:

_____

_____

_____

_____

Behaviour:

_____

_____

_____

| Sketch / Photo |

Weather:_____

Habitat:_____

Notes:_____

_____

_____

_____

Date:_____Time:_____

Location:_____

Bird Species:

_____

Description:

_____
_____
_____
_____

Behaviour:

_____
_____

_____

Sketch / Photo

Weather:_____

Habitat:_____

Notes:_____

_____

_____

_____

Date:_____Time:_____

Location:_____

Bird Species:

_____

Description:

_____

_____

_____

_____

Behaviour:

_____

_____

_____

Weather:_____

Habitat:_____

Notes:_____

Sketch / Photo

Date:_____Time:_____

Location:_____

Bird Species:

_____

Description:

_____

_____

_____

_____

Behaviour:

_____

_____

_____ | Sketch / Photo

Weather:_____

Habitat:_____

Notes:_____

_____

_____

_____

Date:_____Time:_____

Location:_____

Bird Species:

_____

Description:

_____
_____
_____
_____

Behaviour:

_____
_____

_____ | Sketch / Photo

Weather:_____

Habitat:_____

Notes:_____

_____
_____
_____

Date:_____Time:_____

Location:_____

Bird Species:

_____

Description:

_____
_____
_____
_____

Behaviour:

_____
_____

_____

	Sketch / Photo

Weather:_____

Habitat:_____

Notes:_____

Date:_____Time:_____

Location:_____

Bird Species:

_____

Description:

_____
_____
_____
_____

Behaviour:

_____
_____

_____
_____ | Sketch / Photo

Weather:_____

Habitat:_____

Notes:_____
_____
_____
_____

Date:_____Time:_____

Location:_____

Bird Species:

_____

Description:

_____

_____

_____

_____

Behaviour:

_____

_____

_____

_____ | Sketch / Photo

Weather:_____

Habitat:_____

Notes:_____

_____

_____

_____

Date:_____Time:_____
Location:_____
Bird Species:

_____

Description:

_____
_____
_____
_____

Behaviour:

_____
_____

_____ | Sketch / Photo

Weather:_____

Habitat:_____

Notes:_____

_____

_____

_____

Date:_____Time:_____

Location:_____

Bird Species:

_____

Description:

_____

_____

_____

_____

Behaviour:

_____

_____

_____

Weather:_____

Habitat:_____

Notes:_____

_____

_____

_____

Sketch / Photo

Date:_____Time:_____

Location:_____

Bird Species:

_____

Description:

_____

_____

_____

_____

Behaviour:

_____

_____

_____

Weather:_____

Habitat:_____

Notes:_____

_____

_____

_____

Sketch / Photo

Date:_____Time:_____

Location:_____

Bird Species:

_____

Description:

_____

_____

_____

_____

Behaviour:

_____

_____

_____

Sketch / Photo

Weather:_____

Habitat:_____

Notes:_____

_____

_____

_____

Date:_____Time:_____

Location:_____

Bird Species:

_____

Description:

_____

_____

_____

_____

Behaviour:

_____

_____

_____

_____

Weather:_____

_____

Habitat:_____

_____

Notes:_____

_____

_____

_____

Sketch / Photo

Date:_____Time:_____

Location:_____

Bird Species:

_____

Description:

_____

_____

_____

_____

Behaviour:

_____

_____

_____

	Sketch / Photo

Weather:_____

Habitat:_____

Notes:_____

_____

_____

_____

Date:_____Time:_____

Location:_____

Bird Species:

_____

Description:

_____

_____

_____

_____

Behaviour:

_____

_____

_____

	Sketch / Photo

Weather:_____

Habitat:_____

Notes:_____

_____

_____

_____

Date:_____Time:_____

Location:_____

Bird Species:

_____

Description:

_____

_____

_____

_____

Behaviour:

_____

_____

_____

Weather:_____

Habitat:_____

Notes:_____

_____

_____

_____

Sketch / Photo

Date:_____Time:_____

Location:_____

Bird Species:

_____

Description:

_____

_____

_____

_____

Behaviour:

_____

_____

_____

	Sketch / Photo
Weather:_____	
Habitat:_____	
Notes:_____	
_____	
_____	
_____	

Date:_____Time:_____

Location:_____

Bird Species:

_____

Description:

_____

_____

_____

_____

Behaviour:

_____

_____

_____

Weather:_____

Habitat:_____

Notes:_____

_____

_____

_____

Sketch / Photo

Date:_____Time:_____

Location:_____

Bird Species:

_____

Description:

_____

_____

_____

_____

Behaviour:

_____

_____

_____

	Sketch / Photo
Weather:_____	
Habitat:_____	
Notes:_____	

Date:_____Time:_____
Location:_____
Bird Species:

_____

Description:

_____
_____
_____
_____

Behaviour:

_____
_____

_____
                                    Sketch / Photo
Weather:_____

Habitat:_____

Notes:_____
_____
_____
_____

33

Date:_____Time:_____

Location:_____

Bird Species:

_____

Description:

_____

_____

_____

_____

Behaviour:

_____

_____

_____

Weather:_____

Habitat:_____

Notes:_____

_____

_____

_____

Sketch / Photo

Date:_____Time:_____

Location:_____

Bird Species:

_____

Description:

_____

_____

_____

_____

Behaviour:

_____

_____

_____

Weather:_____

Habitat:_____

Notes:_____

_____

_____

_____

Sketch / Photo

Date:_____Time:_____

Location:_____

Bird Species:

_____

Description:

_____

_____

_____

_____

Behaviour:

_____

_____

_____

Weather:_____

Habitat:_____

Notes:_____

_____

_____

_____

Sketch / Photo

Date:_____Time:_____

Location:_____

Bird Species:

_____

Description:

_____
_____
_____
_____

Behaviour:

_____
_____

_____

Weather:_____

Habitat:_____

Notes:_____

Sketch / Photo

Date:_____Time:_____

Location:_____

Bird Species:

_____

Description:

_____

_____

_____

_____

Behaviour:

_____

_____

_____

_____

Sketch / Photo

Weather:_____

Habitat:_____

Notes:_____

_____

_____

_____

Date:_____Time:_____

Location:_____

Bird Species:

_____

Description:

_____

_____

_____

_____

Behaviour:

_____

_____

_____ | Sketch / Photo

Weather:_____

Habitat:_____

Notes:_____

_____

_____

_____

Date:_____Time:_____

Location:_____

Bird Species:

_____

Description:

_____

_____

_____

_____

Behaviour:

_____

_____

_____

Weather:_____

Habitat:_____

Notes:_____

_____

_____

_____

Sketch / Photo

Date:_____Time:_____

Location:_____

Bird Species:

_____

Description:

_____

_____

_____

_____

Behaviour:

_____

_____

_____

Weather:_____   Sketch / Photo

Habitat:_____

Notes:_____

_____

_____

_____

Date:_____Time:_____

Location:_____

Bird Species:

_____

Description:

_____

_____

_____

_____

Behaviour:

_____

_____

_____

Weather:_____

Habitat:_____

Notes:_____

_____

_____

_____

Sketch / Photo

Date:_____Time:_____

Location:_____

Bird Species:

_____

Description:

_____

_____

_____

_____

Behaviour:

_____

_____

_____

| Sketch / Photo |

Weather:_____

Habitat:_____

Notes:_____

_____

_____

_____

Date:_____Time:_____

Location:_____

Bird Species:

_____

Description:

_____

_____

_____

_____

Behaviour:

_____

_____

_____

_____ | Sketch / Photo

Weather:_____

Habitat:_____

Notes:_____

_____

_____

_____

Date:_____Time:_____

Location:_____

Bird Species:

_____

Description:

_____
_____
_____
_____

Behaviour:

_____
_____

_____

Weather:_____

Habitat:_____

Notes:_____

_____
_____
_____

Sketch / Photo

Date:_____Time:_____

Location:_____

Bird Species:

_____

Description:

_____

_____

_____

_____

Behaviour:

_____

_____

_____

Weather:_____

Habitat:_____

Notes:_____

_____

_____

_____

Sketch / Photo

Date:_____Time:_____

Location:_____

Bird Species:

_____

Description:

_____

_____

_____

_____

Behaviour:

_____

_____

_____
                              | Sketch / Photo
Weather:_____ |
                              |
_____ |
Habitat:_____ |
                              |
_____ |
Notes:_____ |
                              |
_____ |
                              |
_____ |
_____ |

Date:_____Time:_____

Location:_____

Bird Species:

_____

Description:

_____

_____

_____

_____

Behaviour:

_____

_____

_____

Weather:_____

Habitat:_____

Notes:_____

_____

_____

_____

Sketch / Photo

Date:_____Time:_____

Location:_____

Bird Species:

_____

Description:

_____

_____

_____

_____

Behaviour:

_____

_____

_____

Weather:_____

Habitat:_____

Notes:_____

Sketch / Photo

Date:_____Time:_____

Location:_____

Bird Species:

_____

Description:

_____

_____

_____

_____

Behaviour:

_____

_____

_____

_____ | Sketch / Photo

Weather:_____

_____

Habitat:_____

_____

Notes:_____

_____

_____

_____

Date:_____Time:_____

Location:_____

Bird Species:

_____

Description:

_____

_____

_____

_____

Behaviour:

_____

_____

_____

Weather:_____

Habitat:_____

Notes:_____

Sketch / Photo

Date:_____Time:_____

Location:_____

Bird Species:

_____

Description:

_____

_____

_____

_____

Behaviour:

_____

_____

_____

_____   Sketch / Photo

Weather:_____

Habitat:_____

Notes:_____

_____

_____

_____

Date:_____Time:_____

Location:_____

Bird Species:

_____

Description:

_____

_____

_____

_____

Behaviour:

_____

_____

_____

Weather:_____

Habitat:_____

Notes:_____

_____

_____

_____

Sketch / Photo

Date:_____Time:_____

Location:_____

Bird Species:

_____

Description:

_____

_____

_____

_____

Behaviour:

_____

_____

_____

| Sketch / Photo |

Weather:_____

Habitat:_____

Notes:_____

_____

_____

_____

Date:_____Time:_____

Location:_____

Bird Species:

_____

Description:

_____
_____
_____
_____

Behaviour:

_____
_____

_____

Weather:_____

Habitat:_____

Notes:_____

_____

_____

_____

Sketch / Photo

Date:_____Time:_____

Location:_____

Bird Species:

_____

Description:

_____
_____
_____
_____

Behaviour:

_____

_____

_____

_____   Sketch / Photo

Weather:_____

Habitat:_____

Notes:_____

_____

_____

_____

Date:_____Time:_____

Location:_____

Bird Species:

_____

Description:

_____
_____
_____
_____

Behaviour:

_____
_____

_____

Weather:_____

Habitat:_____

Notes:_____

_____

_____

_____

Sketch / Photo

Date:_____Time:_____

Location:_____

Bird Species:

_____

Description:

_____
_____
_____
_____

Behaviour:

_____
_____

_____

	Sketch / Photo

Weather:_____

Habitat:_____

Notes:_____

_____
_____
_____

Date:_____Time:_____

Location:_____

Bird Species:

_____

Description:

_____

_____

_____

_____

Behaviour:

_____

_____

_____

Weather:_____

Habitat:_____

Notes:_____

_____

_____

_____

Sketch / Photo

Date:_____Time:_____

Location:_____

Bird Species:

_____

Description:

_____

_____

_____

_____

Behaviour:

_____

_____

_____

	Sketch / Photo
Weather:_____	
Habitat:_____	
Notes:_____	

Date:_____Time:_____

Location:_____

Bird Species:

_____

Description:

_____

_____

_____

_____

Behaviour:

_____

_____

_____

Weather:_____

Habitat:_____

Notes:_____

_____

_____

_____

Sketch / Photo

Date:_____Time:_____

Location:_____

Bird Species:

_____

Description:

_____

_____

_____

_____

Behaviour:

_____

_____

_____

Sketch / Photo

Weather:_____

Habitat:_____

Notes:_____

_____

_____

_____

Date:_____Time:_____

Location:_____

Bird Species:

_____

Description:

_____

_____

_____

_____

Behaviour:

_____

_____

_____

| Sketch / Photo |

Weather:_____

Habitat:_____

Notes:_____

_____

_____

_____

Date:_____Time:_____

Location:_____

Bird Species:

_____

Description:

_____

_____

_____

_____

Behaviour:

_____

_____

_____

Sketch / Photo

Weather:_____

Habitat:_____

Notes:_____

_____

_____

_____

Date:_____Time:_____

Location:_____

Bird Species:

_____

Description:

_____

_____

_____

_____

Behaviour:

_____

_____

_____

	Sketch / Photo

Weather:_____

Habitat:_____

Notes:_____

_____

_____

_____

Date:_____Time:_____

Location:_____

Bird Species:

_____

Description:

_____
_____
_____
_____

Behaviour:

_____
_____

_____

Weather:_____

Habitat:_____

Notes:_____

_____

_____

_____

Sketch / Photo

Date:_____Time:_____

Location:_____

Bird Species:

_____

Description:

_____

_____

_____

_____

Behaviour:

_____

_____

_____

Sketch / Photo

Weather:_____

Habitat:_____

Notes:_____

_____

_____

_____

Date:_____Time:_____

Location:_____

Bird Species:

_____

Description:

_____
_____
_____
_____

Behaviour:

_____
_____

_____

Sketch / Photo

Weather:_____

Habitat:_____

Notes:_____

_____
_____
_____

Date:_____Time:_____

Location:_____

Bird Species:

_____

Description:

_____

_____

_____

_____

Behaviour:

_____

_____

_____ | Sketch / Photo

Weather:_____

_____

Habitat:_____

_____

Notes:_____

_____

_____

_____

Date:_____Time:_____

Location:_____

Bird Species:

_____

Description:

_____

_____

_____

_____

Behaviour:

_____

_____

_____ | Sketch / Photo

Weather:_____

Habitat:_____

Notes:_____

Date:_____Time:_____

Location:_____

Bird Species:

_____

Description:

_____

_____

_____

_____

Behaviour:

_____

_____

_____

Weather:_____

Habitat:_____

Notes:_____

_____

_____

_____

Sketch / Photo

Date:_____Time:_____

Location:_____

Bird Species:

_____

Description:

_____
_____
_____
_____

Behaviour:

_____
_____

_____

Weather:_____

Habitat:_____

Notes:_____

_____
_____
_____

Sketch / Photo

Date:_____Time:_____

Location:_____

Bird Species:

_____

Description:

_____

_____

_____

_____

Behaviour:

_____

_____

_____

_____   Sketch / Photo

Weather:_____

Habitat:_____

Notes:_____

_____

_____

_____

Date:_____Time:_____

Location:_____

Bird Species:

_____

Description:

_____

_____

_____

_____

Behaviour:

_____

_____

_____

	Sketch / Photo

Weather:_____

Habitat:_____

Notes:_____

_____

_____

_____

Date:_____Time:_____

Location:_____

Bird Species:

_____

Description:

_____

_____

_____

_____

Behaviour:

_____

_____

_____

Weather:_____

Habitat:_____

Notes:_____

Sketch / Photo

Date:_____Time:_____

Location:_____

Bird Species:

_____

Description:

_____

_____

_____

_____

Behaviour:

_____

_____

_____ | Sketch / Photo

Weather:_____

Habitat:_____

Notes:_____

_____

_____

_____

Date:_____Time:_____

Location:_____

Bird Species:

_____

Description:

_____

_____

_____

_____

Behaviour:

_____

_____

_____

Weather:_____

Habitat:_____

Notes:_____

_____

_____

_____

Sketch / Photo

Date:_____Time:_____

Location:_____

Bird Species:

_____

Description:

_____

_____

_____

_____

Behaviour:

_____

_____

_____

Weather:_____

Habitat:_____

Notes:_____

Sketch / Photo

Date:_____Time:_____

Location:_____

Bird Species:

_____

Description:

_____

_____

_____

_____

Behaviour:

_____

_____

_____

	Sketch / Photo
Weather:_____	
Habitat:_____	
Notes:_____	
_____	
_____	
_____	

Date:_____Time:_____

Location:_____

Bird Species:

_____

Description:

_____

_____

_____

_____

Behaviour:

_____

_____

_____

| | Sketch / Photo |

Weather:_____

Habitat:_____

Notes:_____

_____

_____

_____

Date:_____Time:_____

Location:_____

Bird Species:

_____

Description:

_____

_____

_____

_____

Behaviour:

_____

_____

_____

Weather:_____

Habitat:_____

Notes:_____

_____

_____

_____

Sketch / Photo

Date:_____Time:_____

Location:_____

Bird Species:

_____

Description:

_____

_____

_____

_____

Behaviour:

_____

_____

_____

Weather:_____

Habitat:_____

Notes:_____

Sketch / Photo

Date:_____Time:_____

Location:_____

Bird Species:

_____

Description:

_____

_____

_____

_____

Behaviour:

_____

_____

_____

Sketch / Photo

Weather:_____

Habitat:_____

Notes:_____

_____

_____

_____

Date:_____Time:_____

Location:_____

Bird Species:

_____

Description:

_____

_____

_____

_____

Behaviour:

_____

_____

_____

Weather:_____

Habitat:_____

Notes:_____

_____

_____

_____

Sketch / Photo

Date:_____Time:_____

Location:_____

Bird Species:

_____

Description:

_____
_____
_____
_____

Behaviour:

_____
_____

_____
_____

Weather:_____

Habitat:_____

Notes:_____

_____

Sketch / Photo

Date:_____Time:_____

Location:_____

Bird Species:

_____

Description:

_____
_____
_____
_____

Behaviour:

_____
_____

_____

Weather:_____

Habitat:_____

Notes:_____

_____

_____

_____

Sketch / Photo

Date:_____Time:_____

Location:_____

Bird Species:

_____

Description:

_____

_____

_____

_____

Behaviour:

_____

_____

_____

Sketch / Photo

Weather:_____

Habitat:_____

Notes:_____

_____

_____

_____

Date:_____Time:_____

Location:_____

Bird Species:

_____

Description:

_____

_____

_____

_____

Behaviour:

_____

_____

_____

Weather:_____

Habitat:_____

Notes:_____

Sketch / Photo

Date:_____Time:_____

Location:_____

Bird Species:

_____

Description:

_____
_____
_____
_____

Behaviour:

_____
_____

_____ | Sketch / Photo
_____ |
Weather:_____ |
_____ |
Habitat:_____ |
_____ |
Notes:_____ |
_____ |
_____ |
_____ |

Date:_____Time:_____

Location:_____

Bird Species:

_____

Description:

_____

_____

_____

_____

Behaviour:

_____

_____

_____

_____

Weather:_____

_____

Habitat:_____

_____

Notes:_____

_____

_____

_____

Sketch / Photo

Date:_____Time:_____

Location:_____

Bird Species:

_____

Description:

_____
_____
_____
_____

Behaviour:

_____
_____

_____

_____   Sketch / Photo

Weather:_____

Habitat:_____

Notes:_____

_____
_____
_____

Date:_____Time:_____

Location:_____

Bird Species:

_____

Description:

_____

_____

_____

_____

Behaviour:

_____

_____

_____

Weather:_____

_____

Habitat:_____

_____

Notes:_____

_____

_____

_____

Sketch / Photo

Date:_____Time:_____

Location:_____

Bird Species:

_____

Description:

_____

_____

_____

_____

Behaviour:

_____

_____

_____

Sketch / Photo

Weather:_____

Habitat:_____

Notes:_____

Date:_____Time:_____
Location:_____
Bird Species:

_____

Description:

_____
_____
_____
_____

Behaviour:

_____
_____

_____   Sketch / Photo

Weather:_____

Habitat:_____

Notes:_____

_____

_____

_____

Date:_____Time:_____

Location:_____

Bird Species:

_____

Description:

_____

_____

_____

_____

Behaviour:

_____

_____

_____

| Sketch / Photo |

Weather:_____

Habitat:_____

Notes:_____

_____

_____

_____

Date:_____Time:_____

Location:_____

Bird Species:

_____

Description:

_____
_____
_____
_____

Behaviour:

_____
_____

_____

Weather:_____

Habitat:_____

Notes:_____

_____

_____

_____

Sketch / Photo

Date:_____Time:_____

Location:_____

Bird Species:

_____

Description:

_____

_____

_____

_____

Behaviour:

_____

_____

_____

_____

Sketch / Photo

Weather:_____

Habitat:_____

Notes:_____

_____

_____

_____

Date:_____Time:_____

Location:_____

Bird Species:

_____

Description:

_____

_____

_____

_____

Behaviour:

_____

_____

_____

| Sketch / Photo |

Weather:_____

Habitat:_____

Notes:_____

_____

_____

_____

Date:_____Time:_____

Location:_____

Bird Species:

_____

Description:

_____

_____

_____

_____

Behaviour:

_____

_____

_____

	Sketch / Photo
Weather:_____	
Habitat:_____	
Notes:_____	
_____	
_____	
_____	

Date:_____Time:_____

Location:_____

Bird Species:

_____

Description:

_____

_____

_____

_____

Behaviour:

_____

_____

_____ | Sketch / Photo

Weather:_____

Habitat:_____

Notes:_____

_____

_____

_____

Printed in Great Britain
by Amazon

85178178R00058